Do Purpose

Why brands with a purpose
do better and matter more.

David Hieatt

CHRONICLE BOOKS
SAN FRANCISCO

To Clare, Stella, and Tessa

First published in the United States of America in 2018 by
Chronicle Books LLC.
First published in the United Kingdom in 2014 by The Do Book Company.

Library of Congress Cataloging-in-Publication Data

Names: Hieatt, David, author.
Title: Do purpose / David Hieatt.
Description: San Francisco : Chronicle Books, [2018]
Identifiers: LCCN 2018000193 | ISBN 9781452171708 (pbk. : alk. paper)
Subjects: LCSH: Branding (Marketing) | Creative ability in business. |
    Success in business.
Classification: LCC HF5415.1255 .H54 2018 | DDC 658.8/27--dc23 LC
record available at https://lccn.loc.gov/2018000193

Manufactured in China.

Cover design by James Victore.
Book designed and set by Nick Hand.

10 9 8 7 6 5 4 3 2 1

Chronicle Books LLC
680 Second Street
San Francisco, California 94107
www.chroniclebooks.com

Contents

FIND YOUR LOVE

The most important brands in the world make you feel something. They do that because there is something they want to change. And as customers, we want to be part of that change.

The founders tell us how the world could be. They bare their soul to us.

These companies have a reason to exist beyond just making a profit: They have a purpose.

Yes, we admire the product they make. But the thing we love the most about them is the change they are making.

We love purpose-driven brands.

SANE PEOPLE QUIT

Starting a business is hard. You'll work like a crazy person and have to sustain that lifestyle over a long period of time. Poor pay. Terrible hours. Tons of stress. Any normal, rational person would quit. And that's what happens. When things get tough—and there will be a point when they do— sane people quit.

But purpose-driven entrepreneurs are different. They fall in love with the change they are making, so they have to find a way to make it work. Their love stops them from quitting. Love makes them persevere.

Love blinkers them to all the worry and stress. And it's their purpose that fuels that love.

CHAPTER ONE
PURPOSE

DRAW THREE CIRCLES

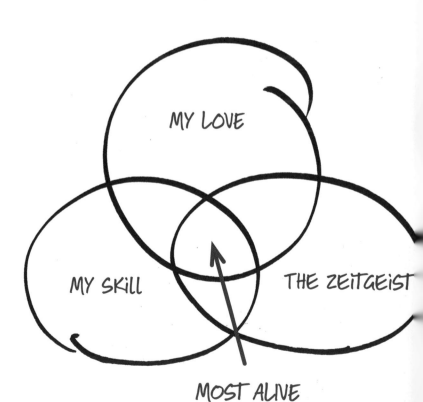

MY LOVE

MY SKILL

THE ZEITGEIST

MOST ALIVE

Here's an exercise to help find your purpose. First, draw three circles.

In the first circle, write what you love doing; in the second circle, write your skill; and in the third one, write what the zeitgeist is.

Where these three circles overlap is where you're most alive. If I were you, I would start a company that lives in this intersection, too. Because the chances of success are greater there. The chances of it making real change are greater. And the chance of it being more fun are greater there, too.

My Love: Does it matter to you? Have you shown an interest in it from an early age?

My Skill: What is it I am good at? And will this startup use my skills fully?

The Zeitgeist*: What have you seen before all the others?

*A trend is the latest fashion, but it may just fade away. A zeitgeist is a shift that will stay shifted.

TWO KINDS OF PASSION

IT'S IMPORTANT TO KNOW WHICH IS WHICH

I think it's helpful to understand passion because purpose-driven companies are mostly built with it.

I believe there are two types of passion. One is "hot passion." It is all heart; the head is not being called upon to think. And that means sometimes things can go wrong. Hot passion is a bit like infatuation—it burns brightly but fades quickly.

Whereas "cold passion" is calm, considered, and long lasting. Both the brain and the heart are working together. Emotions have been taken out of decision making. And decisions are given time, looked at from all angles. Cold passion is much more effective at getting results. Cold passion is like a lifelong love. Once decided upon, it's almost impossible to stop loving.

It's good to be aware of the difference between the two. To be successful, you will need to learn the art of cold passion. You will need to create a discipline where head and heart can both be involved in the decisions that you make. Taking the emotion out of something you feel very passionate about is far from easy. But easy doesn't build great.

DEFINE THE CHANGE THAT YOU WILL MAKE

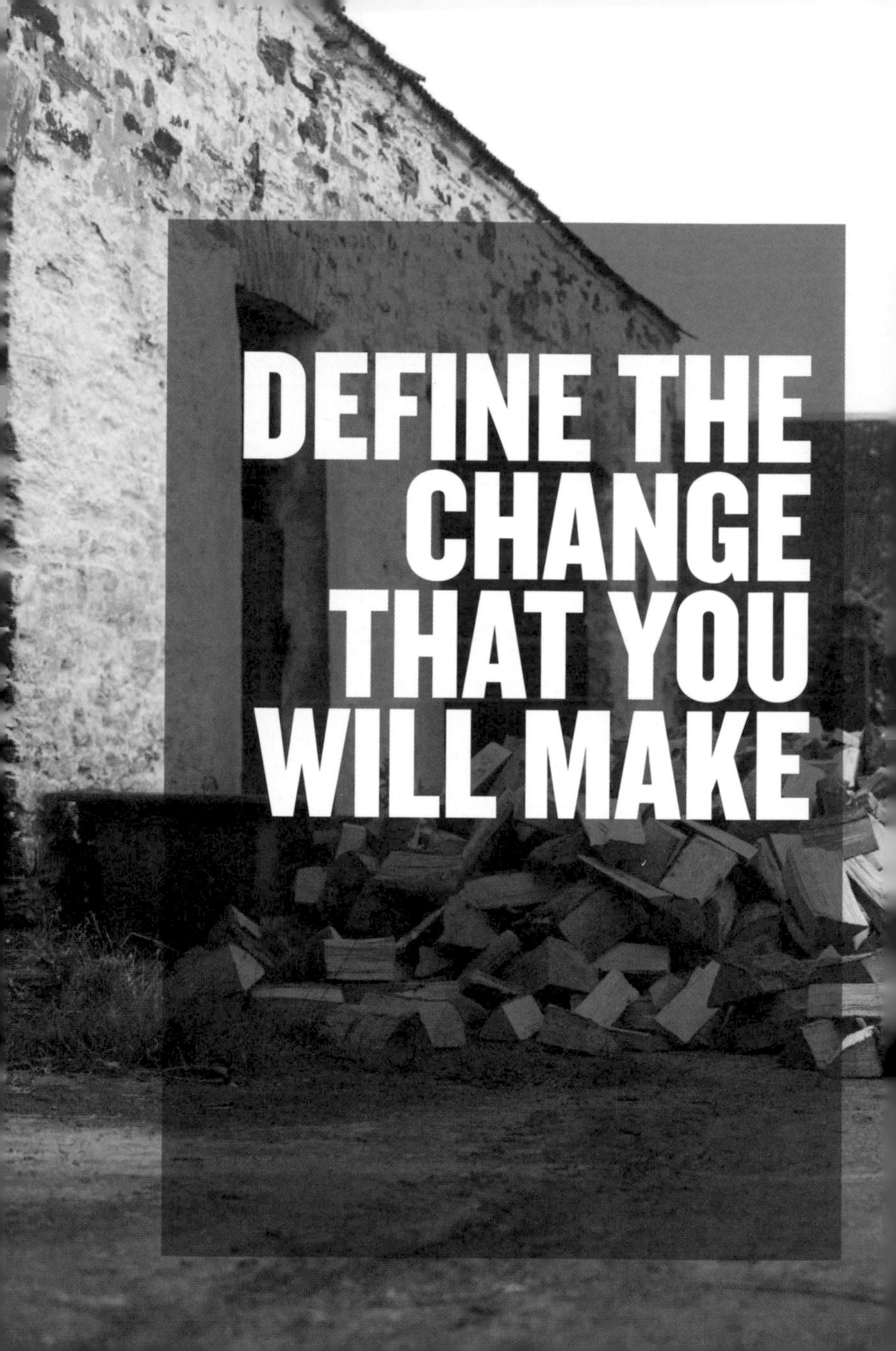

RESPONSIBILITY FOR THE TOTAL

This is the first page from a user manual from an axe company called Gransfors. They know why they are in business: to make axes that last. They want to change a society that thinks throwing away stuff is OK.

"What we take, how and what we make, what we waste, is in fact a question of ethics. We have an unlimited responsibility for the total. A responsibility which we try to take, but do not always succeed in. One part of this responsibility is the quality of the products and how many years the product will maintain its durability. To make a high-quality product is a way to pay respect and responsibility to the customer and the user of the product. A high-quality product, in the hands of those who have learned how to use it and how to look after it, will very likely be more durable. This is good for the owner, the user. But this is good as well as part of a greater whole: increased durability means that we take less (decreased consumption of material and energy), that we need to produce less (gives us more time to do other things we think are important or enjoyable), destroy less (less waste)."

Extract reproduced by kind permission of Daniel Brånby, owner, Gränsfors Bruk.

It doesn't have to be another company. Maybe you need a bigger enemy than just another brand. It can be bad design. It can be time. It can be pollution. It can be ugliness. It can be bad service. It can be landfill. It can be complexity.

This will be your driver, so pick your enemy well. This will become your purpose. Your fuel when you're tired out. Your reason to keep going when others call it a day. It will be why your customer prefers you over all the others. This is your purpose. The thing that separates you from all the others.

The companies that you love today started out with no more money than others; they just had more energy.* Their energy came from how much they wanted to change things. They knew well from day one what their enemy was.

What is your enemy?

*Purpose is the multiplier of energy.

DEFINE YOUR ENEMY

THE COMPETITION HAS MORE OF EVERYTHING THAN YOU

They have more staff. More history. More distribution. More patents. More sales. More infrastructure. More contacts. More marketing. More money. (And they can raise plenty more.)

They have more followers on Instagram, Facebook, Twitter, Pinterest, Medium, and Google+ than you. They spend more on research and development than you turn over as a company. Their coffee budget is bigger than your marketing budget. They never run out of staples; they always have enough photocopier paper; their CEO doesn't have to take out the trash as well as lead the company.

Who would be crazy enough to try and take on a Goliath?

THE COMPETITION HAS MORE OF EVERYTHING THAN YOU

The competition has more meetings. More committees. More red tape. More politics. More internal fighting. More rules. More rules and regulations. More ideas being killed by research than you.

More outdated business models. More unmotivated staff than you. More people wondering "What is this company all about?" than you.

And then there is their legal department: the graveyard of humor and anything else vaguely interesting or pioneering. Who cares if they never run out of staples or photocopier paper? There has never been a better time to be a small company. Don't worry about what they have. You have it all. You have something you want to change.

Brand X

They have customers. They have the past. They have an old business model. They're a commodity. They have to be cheaper. They are the status quo. In recessions, their customers leave and go to the cheapest. They have changed very little and can't remember why they started.

Brand Why

They have fans. They have the future. They have a new business model. They are special. They can charge a premium. They are respected. Their fans love them and they are proud of them. In recessions, their fans stick with them. The people behind Brand Why are changing what they set out to.

YOU CAN'T WONDERFUL PASSING ALL RIGHT.

GET TO
WITHOUT
THROUGH
BILL WITHERS

CALL YOUR HEROES

THEY HAVE A TELEPHONE, TOO

Your heroes have a phone. And a mailbox. And email. Just get in touch and ask them to be your mentor. Remember, they once asked for someone's help. If you tell them what you are trying to change, and it is important to them, too, the chances are they will help you.

Read their books, listens to their talks, read their blogs. They have found a way of making a business out of the thing they love doing. You can learn from them. Suck it all up.

A great mentor can really help you. Aim high.

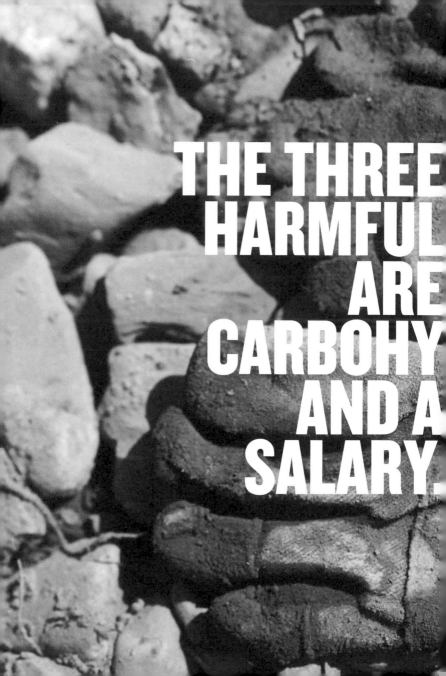

THE THREE HARMFUL ARE CARBOHY AND A SALARY

MOST ADDICTIONS HEROIN, DRATES, MONTHLY

FRED WILSON

WRITE YOUR BUSINESS PLAN ON A DOORMAT

When you order a doormat, they charge per word. This financial restriction makes you think long and hard about what you want to say. The other restriction is that space is limited.

So your thinking needs to be distilled down into the fewest number of words possible. So simple that it can appear on a doormat.

If you could apply the same discipline of writing a doormat to your business plan, I think the chances of you having plenty of customers walking on it would be increased. Why? Because you have no choice but to keep it simple and be clear. And simple and clear are good for business.

So ask yourself what it is that you want to stand for in the fewest number of words that you can:
Kickstarter: *Change Funding of Ideas.*
Patagonia: *Higher Quality. Lower impact.*
Google: *Faster More Relevant Search.*

The less you have to spend on the doormat, the more thinking you have done.

THE BEST BUSINESS MODELS BECOME ROLE MODELS

Look at how Airbnb has changed travel. Look at how Kickstarter has changed how creative ideas get funded. Look at how Zipcar has changed car ownership.

These companies become role models for future businesses. Their real influence will be the companies that get started after them. Their business, and their approach to it, will inspire many more businesses to start. They have shown another way. They have been successful. And people follow success.

Their business models will be studied and no doubt applied to other industries. Their books will be purchased; their opinions will be listened to. They have become influential, important, and inspiring.

Not many companies can say that.

SPEED MATTERS

DIGITAL WORLD

In the tech world, great new companies can be built quickly. They scale big. They scale fast. They scale cheaply. They don't require huge infrastructure. They work best with a small team. They are pioneers. What they are doing has not been done before. They have no map. They are building something fast to get there before their competitor launches. The coder who writes in high-level code is king. Speed matters in this world. How fast you can fix a bug matters. How fast you can add a new feature matters. Patience isn't a virtue here. The need is for speed.

PATIENCE MATTERS

ANALOG WORLD

Take an oak tree. It takes fifty years before you get a single acorn. Who'd invest in one of them? Take writers, take artists, take musicians, take inventors, take photographers, take athletes, take any person from any field you can think of—they all took a decade or more to get good at their thing. In those years, learning was put before earning. In those years, patience was put before any possible shortcut. We live in a very fast one-click world. The time between waking in the morning and looking at a screen is measured in seconds. Our attention span shrinks with each generation. But building a great analog company just takes time.

*DON'T RELY ON GOOD
PRINCIPLES TO SELL
A BAD PRODUCT

BUILD SOMETHING YOU WOULD NEVER SELL

Zach Klein gave a talk at the Do Lectures in Wales. He told the story of building Vimeo from nothing. The fun they had. The team they built. The huge following they amassed. Then, one day, they sold it.

The exit strategy is what every startup is geared up for, and yet after selling Vimeo, he couldn't help but feel that he missed it. The last slide on his talk summed up his learning from his adventures: Build something that you would never sell.

As a founder of a company, you are going to be faced with this dilemma at some point. So here are some questions to ask yourself before you sell: Do you still love it? Is it still fun? And, is the job only half done? If you answer "yes" to these three, my advice would be to keep building.

CHAPTER TWO
TIME

YOUR TIME IS LIMITED. REMEMBER THAT.

Each day, you're given 86,400 seconds from the "Time Bank." Everyone is given the same. There are no exceptions. Once you make your withdrawal, you're free to spend it as you want.

The "Time Bank" won't tell you how to spend it. Time poorly spent will not be replaced with more time. Time doesn't do refunds.

Time is your biggest gift. Indeed, it is more valuable than money, as you can make more money, but you can't make more time. But there is one simple truth: Your time is limited. And one day, you will go to the bank, and it won't have any more for you.

It will be at the exact moment that you will know the answer to this simple question: Did I use my time well? Did I do what mattered most to me? Did I find my love? And did I pursue it like a wild hungry dog?

TURN OFF THE INTERNET

Treat distractions as the enemy. Luckily, each electrical device you have comes with an off button. Remember: your time is limited. But your ability to be distracted is infinite. If you want to get things done, you have to focus. And focus comes from blocking out that busy world out there.

I am not good at email. But I am good at getting things done. I view email as a distraction from making things happen. I view getting things done as more important than having an empty inbox. I have bought all the apps to help me cope with email. But they don't work for me. It's not them. It's me.

The Internet is brilliant, but it is one very efficient way of using your time. It's a super-addictive distraction device that will stop us from getting stuff done if we allow it to.

Just click the off button. You got things to do.

BEGIN BEFORE YOU ARE READY

There's a point on a runway during takeoff that a plane reaches V1 speed. Once it passes V1, it has reached the point of no return. The point where takeoff cannot be aborted. It has to take off. Or crash. In order to determine its V1 speed, every plane will factor in its weight, wind speed, weather conditions, slope, length of runway, and so on. So although there's not a physical line drawn on each runway, it's there.

But when it comes to starting a business, there's no calculation to tell us when the right time is. No marker on a runway for us.

So what happens? We defer. We put barriers up to justify not starting. "The economy isn't great." "I've got a big mortgage." "I need more experience." But as you put those barriers up, only you can tear them down.

There will never be a right time to start. Accept it. So start now.

99% OF BUSINESSES FAIL FOR ONE REASON

They don't start. The start line is the scariest place. Step beyond it, and you can be judged. Step beyond it, and you can fail. Step beyond it, and you can no longer hide behind what might have been.

Most people talk about starting something one day. But "one day" doesn't ever come along. They don't get past the start line. Their ideas are probably good enough to succeed. But their belief isn't strong enough.

The patent office doesn't hold the best ideas. They sit in the back of your head waiting for you to believe in them enough to start.

Once you pass that line, you are in the 1 percent club. Those rare people who turn their ideas into real things. Boom.

SELF-IMPOSED, INSANELY IMPOSSIBLE DEADLINES OFTEN HELP

If you are given a week to get something done, you will take a week. If you are given two weeks, you will take two weeks. Will the one that took two weeks be twice as good? I doubt it. The first week will have been spent sharpening pencils and tidying the office up. (You know it's true.) The second week will be "Hey, we got to get this down." So, both projects had a week of your time, if you think about it.

I doubt there will be a discernible difference between the two except for the time taken to get them done.

Deadlines rule us. That's how we get stuff done. But deadlines shouldn't be easy. If you want to achieve amazing things quickly, set yourself tough, almost impossible deadlines.

And remember: great coffee helps.

WANT TO DO MORE? REST UP

We all want to get as much stuff done as we can, but maybe we are going about it the wrong way.

An experiment in the 1940s measured men loading pig iron onto freight train cars at the Bethlehem Steel Company. The men worked until they'd loaded 12½ tons. By noon, they were exhausted and could do no more.

The next day, they were told to load the pig iron for 26 minutes. Then rest for 34 minutes. They rested more than they worked. At the end of the day, they had each loaded 47 tons. That's almost four times as much as working flat out.

It feels counterintuitive, but a sprint followed by an even longer rest will deliver better results than plodding along for years. Yup, the real badge of honor at work is not to work longer than anyone else, but to work smarter than anyone else.

THE
80/20
RULE

Pareto's law is named after Italian economist Vilfredo Pareto. It is also known as the 80/20 rule, which Richard Koch wrote about in his brilliant book.

The thinking is this: If you run a business, 80 percent of your business probably comes from 20 percent of your customers. If you are a creative person, 80 percent of your awards/recognition/income will come from 20 percent of your output.

So how can knowing this principle help you manage your time? Well, start by looking at your day. See where you spend most of your time.

The likelihood is you will find out most of your time is spent on the things that you are not that good at. Too many meetings. Too much admin. Too much politics. This is called the law of Oterap. (*Pareto* backward.)

You spend 80 percent of your time on the things you are least good at. And where you can make the least difference. You don't need more time in the day. You don't need to work longer hours. You don't need to work weekends. You just need to spend more time on what you are brilliant at . . . and less time on all that other stuff.

BUILDING A GREAT COMPANY JUST TAKES TIME

How we learn.

How we communicate.

What we eat.

How we play.

How we exercise.

Where we live.

How we travel.

Our behavior.

Our governments.

Our corporations.

The music we listen to.

How we relax.

How we stay awake.

The status quo.

The perceived wisdom.

"This is how we do things around here."

IDEAS
CHANGE
EVERYTHING

SOME IDEAS ARE BORN UGLY

Great ideas often have no reference points. We have nothing to compare them to. They are original and awkward. And so they are the most vulnerable to people trying to kill them. They do not conform to what exists, so they challenge us.

So in order to keep a great idea alive, you will have to rely on your gut instinct, which sometimes is the hardest sell of all. You have to believe in your idea when no one else does. The parent has to love the ugly duckling until it turns into a little beauty.

We also judge ideas too quickly. It's not always clear from the beginning which are the good, the bad, and the ugly. Learn not to judge them too quickly. That dumb idea could be the one. If you think conventionally, you may dismiss the ugly duckling.

Great ideas cost no more than rubbish ones. That's nice to know. And, if you want to take the stress out of running a business, have a great idea.

Ideas don't care about who you are or where you are; they don't go to those with the most money or the biggest smile. They come to you in the bath or in the shower, while going for a run, when you least expect it, and when you need them most. But they will come to you. If you would only just listen. And that's a skill you need to learn: always be listening.

A great idea will get you more publicity, give you more energy, and in the end give you more sales. Jake Burton invented a whole new sport: snowboarding. He didn't have a big budget. Just a big idea. A whole new sport.

SMALL BUDGETS REQUIRE BRAVE IDEAS

BE REMARKABLE. (PEOPLE DON'T REMEMBER AVERAGE)

How will you stand out when the world rewards mediocrity? The best way is to not play by their rules.

There's a film called *Mystery Train* by Jim Jarmusch. In the film, a couple of teenage Elvis fans take the tour of the Graceland Mansion. They walk around in awe. The boy has a camera around his neck for the whole tour and yet doesn't take a single photo.

When the couple get back to their cheap studio, the boy starts taking photos of all the lampshades, the cheap furniture, the bad wallpaper. His girlfriend, slightly surprised, asks him why he is taking photographs of all these dumb things when he hadn't taken a single photo all day long.

He said that he would never forget what he had seen at Graceland Mansion, but all this mundane stuff he would soon forget, as it wasn't in any way remarkable. So he was taking photos of it.

IDEAS WORK LIKE VELCRO

Velcro works like this: On one side is a series of hooks going in lots of random directions. On the other side is a series of loops going in lots of random directions. When a hook meets a loop, they connect. It is in the connection business.

It is the randomness of the hooks and the loops that make Velcro work, but they are also important to us if we want to be interesting. We need to have lots of random hooks and loops. If we read the same old books, we get to know more about the thing we know lots about already. We need to subscribe to magazines that we wouldn't normally subscribe to; we need to go to places that we wouldn't normally go to and eat at places that may not be our kind of place.

We stay interesting by stepping outside our groove. We keep pushing; we leave what we know behind for a bit.

This is important from the point of view of coming up with ideas. If your reference points are different from others, then—guess what—your ideas are going to be different. To think differently, you must do differently, read differently, travel differently, eat differently, and so on.

Velcro goes in many different directions in order to make a connection. If we are interested in new ideas, so should we.

Inspired by Russell Davies's "How to Be Interesting" Do Course.

HAVE YOUR RADAR ON

How to identify a niche before others? I think that part of your job as an entrepreneur, as a brand builder, is to always have your radar on. When you see someone doing something odd, it's your job to ask, "What does that mean?" The difference between you and other people is your brain has to think differently. It has to be switched on. It has to notice new behaviors, new patterns, new unanswered needs.

Your eyes and ears will provide most of the answers you will need. You just have to be aware of when they are giving you the answer. To do that, your brain has to be switched on. To spot a star, you have to be looking up at the sky and not down at the floor.

So if you want to spot a niche, always be looking. Watch how people use something. Study people. Listen to people when they say, "I wish someone would . . ."

SOME IDEAS ARE RIGHT IN FRONT OF YOU

Dietrich Mateschitz went on vacation to Thailand and spotted lots of people drinking a native drink called Krating Daeng. He kept asking himself: "What does that mean?" His radar was on. He didn't invent Red Bull. It already existed. He just took something he saw while traveling and turned it into a whole new category.

James Dyson wasn't the only person to walk past a sawmill and see the extractor fan at the top. The answer was available to anyone who asked the right question. But he was the only one to go and make vacuum cleaners using that technology. Yes, it took him five years and more than five thousand iterations. He didn't invent the idea. He took an idea from another industry and applied it to vacuum cleaners. He made it work.

A lot of times the ideas are there right in front of you just waiting for you to take them and put them into another industry or country.

THE FORMULA FOR CHANGE
D×V×F>R

There may not be a formula for ideas, but there is a formula for change. It was created by Richard Beckhard and David Gleicher. The formula provides a model to assess the relative strengths affecting the likely success of a project.

Three factors must be present for meaningful organizational change to take place:

D = Dissatisfaction with how things are now.
V = Vision of what is possible.
F = First, concrete steps that can be taken
    toward the vision.

If the product of these three factors is greater than R (Resistance), then change is possible.

Because D, V, and F are multiplied, if any one is absent or low, then the product will be low and therefore not capable of overcoming the resistance.

It's easy to become comfortable. It's easy to stop pushing. It's easy to do what you did last year. It worked, for goodness' sake.

It is harder to question everything. To walk in dumb each day. To start again with a blank piece of paper.

There is a difference between companies who are always thinking about new ways forward and those who seek to repeat themselves.

Those who repeat themselves have an easy life. But then one day they wake up, and their business is no longer there. The easy life is replaced with a hard life.

Those who keep pushing never have an easy life. They never get to freewheel downhill. They keep cycling like crazy because it is a good mindset for when the hills come. That way of thinking means you never wake up to find the business gone, either.

Tomorrow the reputation has to be made again.

DON'T FREEWHEEL

FALLOW

IDEAS NEED INPUT

FAILURE TO COMMIT IS AS BAD AS FAILURE TO START

Ideas need someone to make them happen. Ideas need doers, not talkers. Ideas require your total belief in them. So before you cross that line, just make sure you are 100 percent into it. Businesses can fail for many reasons.

Perhaps the founders don't quite believe in the idea, or one of the partners loses his or her nerve when the first test comes at them. A lack of belief can be much more damaging than a lack of funding.

In football terms, this is the equivalent of not fully committing in the tackle. And when you are halfhearted in the tackle, you are much more likely to get injured. Players who are saving themselves for the next big game or an important tournament often end up injured because they held back. Holding back often ends in tears.

Likewise, ideas need you to commit. They need all your money. They need all your time. They need all your energy. They need all your love. They need all your belief. If you are halfhearted about the idea, don't even start.

IF YOU'RE GOING TO TRY, GO ALL THE WAY. OTHERWISE, DON'T EVEN START.

CHARLES
BUKOWSKI

23 QUESTIONS TO ASK OF YOUR IDEA

1. Is it a good idea?
2. Is it a new idea?
3. Is it scalable?
4. Will people want it?
5. What change will it bring about?
6. Is it investable?
7. Does it matter to you?
8. Does it matter to your customer?
9. How do you know?
10. How big is the change it can make?
11. Is it good for the planet?
12. Is it good for the human?
13. What is your niche?
14. How big is that niche?
15. How will you test it?
16. Is it a common problem?
17. Does this problem need solving?
18. What disruption will it bring?
19. Where will it be in five years' time?
20. Do you love it?
21. Would you spend ten years doing it?
22. What will its legacy be?
23. Still uncertain about your idea? Keep going. (If not, review your answers to the previous questions and consider what you can improve upon.)

CHAPTER FOUR

BRAND

Have you noticed that you have more ideas when you are not thinking about the thing you should be thinking about? Umm

THE CREATORS CODE

1 Find your love.
2 Spend your life at it.
3 Trust your instincts.
4 Ignore doubters.
5 Chase the work, not the money.
   (The money will come.)
6 Use your ideas to push this world forward.
7 Don't let your ideas down: Execute well.
8 Work with great people. They are not always
   the easiest.
9 There are no shortcuts. Do the hours.
10 Great coffee helps.

Some people think once they have a name and a logo for their company, they have a brand. What they have at that point is just a name and a logo. No more.

The job of the brand is to make that name and that logo stand for something. To live its founding principles each day. To stay true. How do you do that? Well, by making a great product, giving a great service, and by using your company as the tool to change the things that you said you would. It's not difficult. Just hard.

Of course, a good name and a good logo help. But do you think Apple would have made it if they were called Peach? Of course they would have.

I think of a brand as consistent promise. "I promise to make the best running shoes on the planet." "I promise to provide a faster more relevant search." "I promise to make the highest quality outdoor clothing with the least amount of harm to the planet." What's your promise? Your promise is your brand.

A BRAND ISN'T JUST A NICE LOGO

HOW TO GET PEOPLE TO LOVE YOUR BRAND

I get asked this a lot. And there is a surprisingly simple answer: You have to love it the most first. That's it? Yeah, that's it.

This is a "labor of love." And you're the "labor" they are referring to. You have to sweat each detail. Over and over again. Relentlessly paying obsessive attention to the littlest teeny weeny bit. And guess what: your customers will notice. They will see that you have poured your heart into it, and they will love that you care that much about them.

At every stage, you will have put the customer first. Always. Don't let bean counters cut quality in order to improve margins. Long-term relationships with your customers should never be sacrificed for short-term profits. It is much easier to find a new bean counter than a new customer.

The customer can tell when a company loves its customers. And that love is felt and appreciated. Love scales.

This is a story I was told about Ralph Lauren.
It may or may not be true.

Anyway, the story goes like this: Ralph Lauren
spent millions building his ranch. Every detail
considered. The builders and the architects had
a tough old time of it. It was redone a couple
of times. After it was finally finished, they
were super happy. But, for Ralph, something
was missing. Something wasn't quite right.
Eventually, he figured it out: The door was too
perfect. It didn't squeak. And everyone knows
old ranches always have a squeaky door. So the
builders had to put one in.

Imagine how much detail is considered for
his clothes.

A brand is about consistency. Each detail paid
attention to. Because consistency builds trust.
And trust builds a business. And, as the founder,
it is your job to be the guardian of these details.
What matters? Only everything.

THE ONLY THING THAT MATTERS IS EVERYTHING

REPUTATIONS TAKE DECADES TO MAKE—AND ONE WASH TO LOSE

The first clothing company I started had a reputation for making excellent merino base layers. The margin wasn't the best, but we never had to go to sale. We couldn't get enough of it. But a buyer had seen the margin—and wanted to improve it.

The buyer's way of improving it was to buy an inferior quality grade of merino. It was, of course, a better margin. We all tried it. And it was simply not good enough. The merino became saggy after just one wash. As soon as I saw this, I stopped it. But the buyer couldn't understand it. The buyer even tried to bypass me in order to purchase behind my back. I stopped that, too.

For me, there is no point in achieving a great margin once, only to lose that customer after one wash. Your brand reputation should never be compromised for a short-term gain.

YOUR VOICE CAN BE MANY THINGS

I sat down for a coffee with Richard, one of the founders of Innocent Drinks, a UK-based company that makes juices and smoothies, and he told me his taxi story. He was taking a ride back to work, I think. Anyway, as all taxi drivers do, his driver wanted to make conversation. His went along normal lines. "What do you do, mate?" Richard replied, "I help run a smoothie company." "Oh, yeah, which one?" "Innocent." "Nice company. But it's not the same any more." Richard was a bit taken aback. "How do you mean?" "Well, you changed the label. It's glossy now, and the other one was matte. So it doesn't feel as real any more—you know, as authentic." Richard thanked him once he was dropped off. And he went into work, and the first thing he did was change the label back from glossy to matte.

The taxi driver had just taught him the importance of the bigness of small. How those little things that we don't think are that important have a huge impact. If you want to build something big, do all the small things right.

HOW MANY SENSES DOES YOUR BRAND USE?

A brand should appeal to all your senses. But most brands appeal only to sight and sound. They leave touch, smell, and taste alone. And yet, they can be very powerful. Abercrombie and Fitch spray each catalog with their perfume. It acts as a reminder when you walk into the stores. Jawbone portable speakers sound like a futuristic spaceship taking off when you switch one on. If you want to be convinced of its state-of-the-art technology, just turn one on. It is quite something.

The chef Ferran Adrià believes that taste is not the only sense a chef should appeal to, which is interesting. Touch can be played with through various temperatures, as can smell and sight. To him, the senses become one of the main points of reference in the creative process.

It isn't just coffee shops that can tap the power of the sense of smell. It isn't just chefs who can tap the power of the sense of taste. And it isn't just clothing companies who can tap into the power of the sense of touch. Is your brand using all our senses?

MAKE THEM FEEL SOMETHING FOR THE CHANGE YOU'RE MAKING

The best brands not only change something, they also have a great innate ability to communicate their purpose well, so it matters to their customers.

You have to make your customers feel something for the change you are making, or you will change very little. Understand what is in their hearts. Logic is a blunt tool in this regard. It makes perfect sense, it checks all the boxes, but it changes very little. And guess what: Intelligence is no better; it is overrated in its ability to either change things or behavior. I think one of the best ways to leave your customers inspired, stirred, and awoken is to use emotion. Make them feel something.

Bare your soul. Tell your struggle. Tell your pain. Tell your lows. Be vulnerable. Be honest. Tell them how the world could be.

But most of all, be you.

YOUR VOICE
BE CONSISTENT WITH IT

A worthwhile business has to be built over time. A company's product, its purpose, and how it speaks to the world need to be consistent if it wants to be everything that it hopes to be.

So do not blow with the wind. Do not chase a bandwagon. Stay true. Patience is required in a world that doesn't always understand the value of it. It is easy to make little changes in a busy day and think they do not matter. But there is a bigness to small decisions.

The financial world fully understands the concept of compound interest and how a small change can make a big difference. Similarly, a small tweak here or a small compromise there can accumulate over time to change the very soul of a business.

The rule of consistent product and service are understood by everyone. But the same rule needs to be applied to a company's voice. Nike has talked with the same voice for a couple of decades now. A signature message and tone seems to run through it.* And because it is so consistent, each communication seems to build on top of the last one. The company has gained compound interest of voice thanks to its consistency of voice.

*Nike owes their advertising agency, Wieden + Kennedy, a little something.

A brand is a story. And you have to tell it well. The good news in this connected world is that great stories travel fast. And, these days, they travel for free. So there has never been a better time or a cheaper time to start something. Big companies no longer have a huge advantage. Your website can make you look as big as them. Your Instagram can make you funnier than them; your tweets can make you look more human than them.

The tools at your disposal are very powerful and very free. Tools like StumbleUpon (free), Medium (free), Instagram (free), Facebook (free), Twitter (free). Digital cameras—they get cheaper with each season.

Your ability to make a great, unique product will need to be matched by your ability to tell your story. Don't take a quick picture; take a considered one. Don't write an okay blog; spend days writing a great one. Don't make a film that is good when a great one just takes a little more sweat.

Do the work.
Tell your story well.

We live in a very busy world. We have the same amount of time as before, but there are so many more things are competing for our attention. What gets it? The things that stand out. "Average" sinks to the bottom. Fast.

Average viral films don't get shared. Average Instagrams posts don't get liked. Boring tweets don't get retweeted. Social media takes no prisoners. It's binary. You either have our attention or you don't. It's ruthless in sorting out the good from the bad.

The good thing is this: Excellent costs no more than average. In fact, you can argue that average costs more than excellent. All the money and effort to make something that no one is going to see is a dumb waste of money. The answer is to spend more time on being creative. It will pay you back in spades.

"AVERAGE" DIES FASTER THAN EVER BEFORE

Ever been to a great restaurant where the waiter was just plain not interested? Ever been in a famous shop when the salesman chatted to his friends on the phone the entire time you were in the shop? Ever been to a five-star hotel and the service was darned awful? It doesn't matter who you are; if you hire people who don't care, they will do their very best to reveal it to your customers.

And all that work you have put in gets crushed. So when you hire, ask yourself this: Are they passionate about what you are about? Are they a good fit with your brand and its principles? When you walk in the door at Abercrombie & Fitch, it soon becomes very clear what is "on brand" for them.

The people you hire will represent you when you are not there. Does that frighten you or comfort you?

YOUR PEOPLE ARE YOUR BRAND

CHAPTER FIVE

PEOPLE

TEAMS
GATHER
AROUND
CHANGE

Your purpose will define your product. The culture of your company. The people you hire. Even the customers who buy from you. And ultimately, it will define how successful you are. But perhaps the most important thing that your purpose gives everyone in the company is a clear understanding of why the company exists. Everyone in the company understands what it is that you are going to change.

Change is your secret fuel. People want to be part of change. People want to be part of history. Teams gather around ideas that will change things.

That's why your purpose matters. It builds teams who are passionate about the project. They are there to make a difference, not just to make a quick buck.

When a team is motivated, when a team understands the change it will make—even when the odds are stacked against it—it is an impossible thing to stop.

TEAMS BUILD A BUSINESS. CULTURE BUILDS A TEAM.

A company is only as strong as the people who work in it. The people are only as strong as the culture that exists within the company. And the purpose of the company, its reason to exist, will define the culture.

Culture is a funny thing to talk about. You can't see it. You can't feel it. But when it's not right, you can both see it and feel it. Culture is not a big thing. Just lots of small things.

Patagonia lets their people go surfing when the surf is good. At my Hiut Denim Co, every pair of jeans is signed by the Grand Masters who made them: All artists sign their work. Nike created a group called the EKINs. They know Nike backward. Some even had a tattoo to show they were part of the elite.

When you define your purpose, it attracts like-minded people as moths to a flame to light. So define it well.

Your culture will attract your people. Nike started life as a company that sold running shoes. It was founded by a runner and a running coach. Its first employee was Jeff Johnson. He was a runner, too. That was its culture. They wanted to change running.

Johnson created the first product brochures, print ads, and marketing materials, and he even shot the photographs for the company's catalogs. He established a mail-order system and opened the first store. He also designed several early Nike shoes and even conjured up the name *Nike* in 1971.

Even more than doing all this, he wrote letters to athletes to see how things were going with training. When it came to the Olympics, and athletes had to choose between wearing Adidas or Nike, they chose the one who had taken an interest in their running. Those letters changed Nike's history.

Who is going to be your first hire?

EMPLOYEE NUMBER 1

HIRE SLOWLY

Make the interview last longer. An hour is not enough. You will get to know more about potential employees by assigning them a live project. Give them a short deadline. See how they fare. It will tell you so much more than an interview* ever will.

Take them out of the office. Go for a run with them. Have a beer with them. See them as people. If you can't spend time with them, do you really want to hire them?

Remember, a crazy amount of your management time will be spent on a wrong hire. A lot of your stress will come from having to deal with a wrong hire. So can you afford to spend more of your time on making the hiring process longer? Yup, I think so.

*Introverts don't interview well but can have the best ideas.

FIRE QUICKLY

Not every hire works out. And both parties know it quickly. Within three months, you know that ... well ... it isn't going to end well. And yet companies don't act. The person isn't happy. The team isn't happy.* And that can last for years. Decades, even.

Your duty is to the team, to the culture, and, ultimately, to the purpose of the company. And, therefore, you have to do the difficult thing quickly.

The person would be happier in another job. The team would be happier with another person. And life is too short for people to be miserable. People make the mistake of being nice and not dealing with the problem. This means the person is unhappier for longer. It may seem counterintuitive, but there is a kindness to acting quickly.

*A players prefer to be around A players.

NO ASSHOLE RULE

One way to break a team is to hire someone who is talented but who will destroy the team spirit. Because of their talent, people like this have been indulged in other companies. They have been allowed to be monsters. They are out for themselves. And they will do anything they can to win. But the one thing they won't do is to put the team first.

We have all played soccer with a talented player who can do everything with the ball at his feet but pass it to his teammates. He may score a great goal, but the team will lose the game.

A good friend told me the story of seven matchsticks. How each one on its own could be snapped. But when you join them together, no one can break them. The most talented people know they can't do it alone. Teams win.

HIRE HUNGER OVER TALENT

In an ideal world, you would have both hunger and talent in one person. Alas, that isn't always possible. So if you had to choose between the two, I would choose hunger.

Hunger is always keen to learn. Always trying to get better. Hunger is always putting the extra hours in. Hunger doesn't get lazy.

Over time, hunger works so hard at his thing that his talent begins to shine above even someone with a natural gift for it. Hunger is normally insecure about his talent. So he continues to work at it. He never loses the hunger. So he just keeps putting the practice in. Malcolm Gladwell believes "Talent is the desire to practice." I am pretty sure he is right about that.

Indeed talent is the result of the hunger to get better. You can't give people hunger. You can't train it or inspire it. "A person either has hunger in his belly or not. It comes with him when he walks into the room."

I agree with the Real Madrid chairman when he speaks about his soccer team: Expensive is cheap. His point is that buying a $100 million player was better value than buying a $14 million player. The galácticos (superstars) sold more shirts, got more press, and did more for the "Real Madrid" brand around the world. The $14 million players did none of these things, so he deemed them expensive.

I am figuring you don't have millions to burn on talent. But if you want to succeed, you will have to work with the best.

So whether it's a website builder, a photographer, a designer, a hacker, tell them your small budget means they can have creative freedom. The one thing creative people want is to show the rest of the world how creative they are. So you can't give them lots of money, but you can give them lots of freedom. Let them fly. They live to fly.

WORK WITH THE BEST

ESPECIALLY IF YOU'RE AN UNDERFUNDED START-UP

BUILD A VIRTUAL TEAM

In start-up, mode you can't hire all the team members you want from day one. But you know who they are, right? You've been admiring their work for years.

So how can you get them on the team? Write to them. Show them pictures of their work in your scrapbook. And tell them your mission. And tell them the change you will make.

Recently I was working with our graphic designer Nick Hand on the Yearbook for Hiut Denim Co. He came in with a book from a famous graphic designer and illustrator in New York (James Victore). I loved his work. His work was already in my scrapbooks. "We need to work with people as good as him," said Nick.

I was thinking, "We don't need to work with people like him. We need to work *with* him." So somehow I found out his email. And I wrote to him. I told him my town was going to make jeans again. And if we wanted to get everybody their jobs back, we would have to be brilliant. And that meant we could only work with the best. So we had to work with him. He wrote back and said "I'm in."* If I had looked at our budget, I would never have sent him the email.

*He also designed the cover for this book.

MAKE YOUR COMPANY A PLACE TO LEARN

People don't leave companies for money.
They say they do. But they don't.

They leave emotionally long before they leave physically. They leave because they are not valued, they are not being challenged, or they do not feel part of something that matters to them. A central plank to all this discontent is that they have stopped learning.

It's your job to create a learning culture that will keep them emotionally connected. You have to keep their hearts in the business. Training is the best way I know to do that.

And it isn't just training to do their job better. That's standard stuff. You will need to go beyond that to get people engaged.

You will need to send them on courses, even if that course is unrelated to what they do with you. The best companies see the whole person, and not just the little segment that that person does for you.

THE ONLY THING WORSE THAN TRAINING YOUR EMPLOYEES AND HAVING THEM LEAVE IS NOT TRAINING THEM AND HAVING THEM STAY.

HENRY FORD

TRUST

Tina Roth Eisenberg (better known as @swissmiss) gave a talk at Do Lectures USA. She talked a lot about building her amazing companies, building the team, and the importance of fun. One of the slides that she put up read: "Trust breeds **magic**."

Yup, like Tina, I believe in teams. I believe when a team comes together, there is very little that it can't do. But some teams end up fighting each other like crazy, and subsequently, they go the way of the dinosaur. This fascinates me. So why do some teams come together and others fall apart?

I know, in order to build a business, I have to build a team first. It is one of the key skills that an entrepreneur has to learn.

BREEDS

Building a team isn't complex. My experience tells me that a team is galvanized by two things. First, they like to gather around the founding idea of the company. The more that idea is going to change things, the more people will want to gather around it. Purpose is important.

The second thing teams love to gather around is a leader they trust. Trust is a multiplier of energy for a team. In order for the team to trust the leader, the leader has to show the team that he or she trusts them. Trust is a two-way street.

But most companies are not set up to trust their people. In fact, they are set up to do the opposite. And yet trust is free. It breeds loyalty and passion and helps pull us all together. The magic of trust is that it helps a team become a team.

CHAPTER SIX

YOU

PLAY THE LONG GAME

The problem with a purpose-driven company is that it matters to you.

And, oh boy, it can and will consume you. Every waking hour. Every sleeping hour. At home. At work. And the journey between the two.

That's the deal. But you have to find ways to look after yourself. Because you look after lots of other people who depend on you.

Accept that working through the night is a rite of passage, and working weekends goes with the territory. But also accept that these can't become the norm.

Tired? Go home. Come in fresh. Businesses are very good at running you. Don't let it.

SLEEP IS THE MULTIPLIER OF ENERGY

Great businesses are built on huge amounts of energy. And huge amounts of energy are more important than huge amounts of funding.

You can burn the candle at both ends for a while, but there comes a point where you get diminishing returns.

You job is to lead. Your job is to make decisions. Your job is to be a bundle of energy and enthusiasm.

It may sound boring, but if you are going to give your company its best chance of success, you need to get the amount of sleep that your body requires. There is no badge of honor the person for who is the most tired.

IF YOU WANT A GUARANTEE, BUY A TOASTER

Some advice: If you worry a lot, starting a business may not be for you. It doesn't come with a guarantee. Things rarely go as per business plan. And each day comes with a new challenge.

So what are the tricks to stop yourself from worrying?

First, write down on a plain piece of paper "What is the worst that can possibly happen?" Is it that I will lose this house? Is it loss of reputation? Is it fear of failure? And accept that before you start. If you can't accept it, don't start.

READ
THIS
BOOK

Dale Carnegie wrote a book all about dealing with worry. He noticed businessmen were dying of stress-related illnesses. He did some research in his local library. There were forty-seven books on worms. And just one on worry. That made him worry so much that he went and wrote a book all about it.

Carnegie's book may have been written a half a century ago, but it has some nuggets of gold among its pages. Before you set off and start your thing, give yourself some techniques to help you cope with worry.

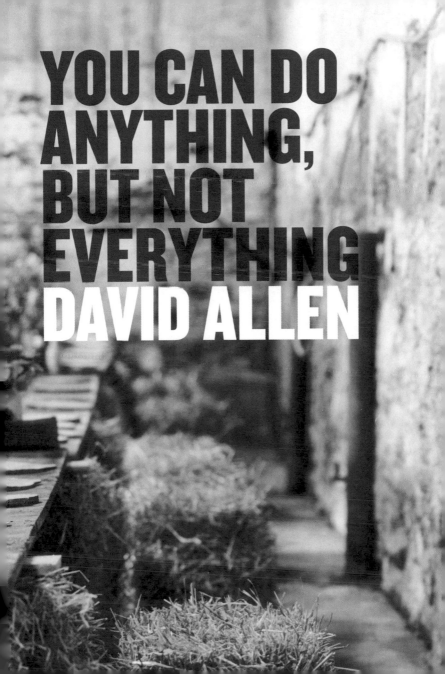

FIND ANOTHER DISTRACTION

Lots of people who run a business find it hard to switch off. That is because they are obsessive control freaks. Nothing wrong with that, by the way.

One way to switch off is to find something else to obsess over. Take up a sport or get a hobby and obsess over that. Take up golf, fishing, yoga, tool making, baking bread, and so on.

While you're obsessing over your hobby, you can take your mind off the business—it may give you ideas that will help you. Sometimes the best way to have ideas is to be thinking of something else.

Sport is important. Whatever you do, take time out. Whether it's a run, a walk, a bike ride, or daily meditation.

The brain needs some rest. Work the body, and while the body is so busy doing its stuff, the brain switches off.

You feel fresher physically and mentally. Feel the burn of sport. There are no emails to send, no bills to pay, no awkward people conversations. You are free.*

Sport takes the stress of the day away and leaves it far behind.

*And free is a good place to go to as often as you can.

LIFE IS COMPLICATED, BUT SPORT IS SIMPLE.

NATURE
LIKES
BALANCE

The bodies and minds that work for you need balance too. When you are involved in a start-up, life can quickly go out of control. If you allow it to. Yes, there will be times when a deadline means burning the midnight oil. And yes, adrenaline is the fuel of start-ups but mostly because it is cheap. But not because it is the best fuel to build a long-term business.

So your job is to look after the team because your team members look after the business. So you have to make sure that those crazy times do not become the norm. You have to create a culture where people take their holidays; where late nights are the exception; where people eat well, sleep well, and use their time well. (Read David Allen's *Getting Things Done*. It is a secret weapon.)

Your team members are more creative, think better, and are much more fun to be around, too, if you can create a culture of balance.

DO ONE THING WELL

IT'S ENOUGH.